PRIMARY
LANGUAGE LESSONS

BY

EMMA SERL

TEACHER, NORMAL TRAINING DEPARTMENT

KANSAS CITY, MO.

LOST CLASSICS BOOK COMPANY

PUBLISHER

LAKE WALES

FLORIDA

Publisher's Note

Recognizing the need to return to more traditional principles in education, Lost Classics Book Company is republishing forgotten late 19th and early 20th century literature and text books to aid parents in the education of their children.

This edition of *Primary Language Lessons* was reprinted from the 1911 copyright edition. The text has been updated and edited only where necessary.

———+———

Library of Congress Catalog Card Number: 96-76987
ISBN 0-9652735-1-2

Primary Language Lessons has been assigned a reading level of 490L. More information concerning this reading level assessment may be obtained by visiting www.lexile.com.

PREFACE

THE object of this little volume is to lead children of the second and third grades into the habit of speaking and writing the English language correctly. To accomplish this, the author has prepared a drill book which emphasizes the reproduction of many of the short stories current in our literature, and also introduces practice exercises to familiarize the pupils with correct forms. Beginning with simple, graduated exercises, they are continued till a general principle is inductively reached.

It is assumed that the child will learn to speak and write correctly, by imitation, if the proper forms are presented to him. Accordingly much attention is given in this book to expressions frequently misused, as for example, troublesome verb forms. The lessons are designed, as well, to awaken and sustain children's interest in natural objects, and to put them in sympathetic relations with living things.

The author has written from the standpoint of the child, and in language that the child can readily comprehend. The book, too, is so unconventional that the Suggestions to Teachers, which follow, are all that is necessary to guide the novice in the successful use of it.

J. M. GREENWOOD

KANSAS CITY, MO.

SUGGESTIONS TO TEACHERS

THIS book is intended for use with pupils of the second and third grades.

Assignment of lessons. — It is not intended that each lesson shall represent one day's work. The intelligent teacher, knowing the capabilities of her pupils, can best determine the amount of work that should be done. Some of the lessons will doubtless require part of the recitation periods of many days.

Dictation exercises. — In giving a dictation exercise, the teacher should read each sentence once. The sentences in the exercises have been made short so that they can be retained easily in the pupil's memory. The results of the pupil's work should be carefully noted by the teacher, attention being called to mistakes in spelling, capitalization, and punctuation, or to failure to reproduce the *exact words dictated*.

Careful work in these dictated exercises and frequent drills on the lists containing "troublesome words" are *sure* to produce good results in written composition.

Selections to be memorized. — These selections should be read to the pupils and discussed with them before being memorized. The *November* poem, *The Brown Thrush*, and *The Bluebird* should be taught at appropriate seasons of the year.

Drawing. — Several exercises are given in drawing.

iv

The purpose is not to obtain finely finished pictures, but to secure the representation of ideas. Let the pupils select the central theme of the pictures to be drawn, and then decide on a fitting background and surroundings.

Pictures. — Most of the pictures used in this book are copies of the works of great artists. A few suggestive questions are given with each picture, but the teacher should supplement these with many others.

Nature and observation lessons. — These lessons should be introduced by oral discussions covering the points indicated by the questions or directions. After the discussion, a pupil should read the question silently, and then give the answer aloud as a complete sentence. As the class progresses, these answers may be written, but they should always be preceded by the oral discussion.

Lessons on troublesome forms. — These lessons should be repeated many times, not at a single period or at succeeding ones, necessarily, but at different times during the year. A little quick work on preceding lessons fixes important forms as no single treatment can do.

Lesson 86 should be repeated many times until the expressions, "It is I" and "It is he," no longer seem strange. This exercise may be read by two pupils, and the answers given from memory.

Variety may be given to this line of work by having pupils occupy different positions about the room, the teacher asking questions that will require the use of these forms in the answer; as, "Who is at the blackboard?" "It is I," "It is she," or "It is he."

This book in the hands of the pupils makes possible much review work that cannot be given when each lesson must be written on the board by the teacher.

The teacher should keep a record of the most common errors committed by the pupils, and should give frequent drills on sentences containing the correct forms.

The best results in the use of good English come from *continued practice on correct forms* rather than from the learning of many rules.

Every lesson should be a language lesson. No mistake in grammar, pronunciation, or in the use of a word should pass uncorrected.

CONTENTS

xi

PIPER AND NUTCRACKERS

LESSON 1

A PICTURE LESSON

What do you see in the picture?
Where are the squirrels?
What are they doing?
What season of the year is it?
What is the bird doing?
Tell about some squirrels that you have seen.
Where did they live?
How did they prepare for winter?
What is the name of the picture?
What is the name of the artist who painted

LESSON 2

Copy the following:
Two squirrels lived in a hollow tree. They had a pleasant home. The leaves shaded them. Sometimes the birds sang to them.
In the fall the frost came. The nuts fell to

the ground. The leaves became red and yellow. The days grew colder.

Then the squirrels gathered nuts and seeds and put them away for winter.

Write the first three lines from dictation.

LESSON 3

IS — ARE

Copy these sentences, filling each blank with *is* or *are:*

1. Two squirrels _____ in the tree.
2. A little bird _____ singing to them.
3. There _____ green leaves around them.
4. The blue sky _____ above them.
5. Nuts _____ ripe and the squirrels _____ happy.

Copy from your reader two sentences that contain the word *is.*

Copy two sentences that contain the word *are.*

LESSON 4

SELECTION TO BE MEMORIZED

If I Knew

If I knew a box where the smiles are kept,
　　No matter how large the key
Or strong the bolt, I would try so hard
　　'Twould open, I know, for me;
Then over the land and the sea broadcast,
　　I'd scatter the smiles to play,
That the children's faces might hold them fast
　　For many and many a day.

If I knew a box that was large enough
　　To hold all the frowns I meet,
I would like to gather them every one,
　　From nursery, school, and street;
Then folding and holding, I'd pack them in,
　　And turning the monster key,
I'd hire a giant to drop the box
　　To the depths of the deep, deep sea.

— Maud Wyman

LESSON 5

OBSERVATION LESSON

Frost

When does the frost come?

What does the frost do to plants?

What plants are killed first by the frost?

Which plants last the longest in the fall?

What plants and trees cannot grow where you live, on account of the frost?

What does the frost do to nut burs?

What effect has it upon the air?

LESSON 6

FOR DICTATION

The moon is round and bright.

It shines at night.

The sun gives light to the moon.

The moon gives light to us.

It is not so far away as the stars.

The moon and the stars make the night beautiful.

LESSON 7

SELECTION TO BE MEMORIZED

A SECRET

We have a secret, just we three,
The robin and I and the sweet cherry tree;
The bird told the tree, and the tree told me,
And nobody knows it but just us three.

But of course the robin knows it best,
Because she built the — I shan't tell the rest,
And laid the four little — somethings in it —
I'm afraid I shall tell it every minute.

With what kind of letter is the word *I* always written?

LESSON 8

Copy these sentences and fill the blanks by referring to Lesson 7.

The robin and I and _____ _____ _____ have a secret.

The bird told _____ _____.

_____ _____ told me.

Nobody knows it but _____ _____ _____.

_____ _____ knows the secret best.

LESSON 9

FOR DICTATION

THE CLOUDS

Clouds float in the sky.
They bring the rain and the snow.
Sometimes they hide the sun.
Sometimes they hide the moon and the stars.

With what kind of letter does the first word in every sentence begin?

LESSON 10

REPRODUCTION — ORAL

THE DOG IN THE MANGER

A dog lay in a manger in which was placed hay for the oxen.

At noon the oxen came to eat their dinner.

The dog growled and snapped at them, and would not let them have even a mouthful.

"You selfish fellow," said an ox, "you cannot eat the hay. Why won't you let us have it?"

From a painting by Adam.

WIDE AWAKE

LESSON 11

A PICTURE LESSON

What do you see in the picture?

Where are the kittens?

If you had three kittens like these, what would you name them?

What is the name of this picture?

What is the artist's name?

Tell a story about the kittens.

LESSON 12

OBSERVATION LESSON

Read each question silently, and give the answer as a complete statement.

With what is a cat covered?
Of what use is the fur?
When is the fur thickest?
When does a cat shed its fur?
What does a cat eat?
Of what use is a cat about a house or barn?
Of what use are the soft cushions or pads on a cat's feet?
Of what use are the claws?
How many claws has a cat on each forefoot? How many on each hind foot? Why does a cat need more claws on her forefeet than on her hind ones? Where are the claws when not in use? How does Puss keep them sharp?
What is the shape of the center of a cat's eye when she has been in the dark? How does it look when she has been in a strong light?
What kind of teeth has a cat?

Tell something about a cat's tongue.

Of what use are a cat's whiskers?

How does a cat carry her little ones? How does she keep them clean?

Is it easy to teach a cat tricks?

LESSON 13

COMPOSITION

Write answers to the first six questions about the cat, in Lesson 12.

LESSON 14

CONVERSATION LESSON

THE CARE OF PETS

If you had a pony, how would you take care of him?

What would you give him to eat?

What does a pony need besides food?

Tell some things that should *not* be done to a pony.

What could the pony do for you?

How would you take care of a canary bird?

What could a canary bird do in return for your care?

What care does a dog require?

What could a dog do for you?

Do you know any story about a dog's helping someone?

What tricks can you teach a dog?

What other animals are good pets?

Tell how to take care of them.

How many questions are there in this lesson?

What mark of punctuation is placed after each question?

LESSON 15

FOR COPYING AND DICTATION

TO — TOO — TWO

1. Two pints make one quart.
2. This work is not too hard for me.
3. Mother sent me to the store.

4. She told me to buy some meat, and some eggs, too.

5. Two boys went to the river.

LESSON 16

Copy these sentences, filling the blanks with *to, too,* or *two.*

1. _____ boys were flying a kite.
2. It is not _____ cold _____ play in the yard.
3. _____ squirrels live in the old oak tree.
4. The children like _____ watch them.
5. Do not go _____ close _____ the edge of the pond.
6. Mary went _____ church, and her sister went, _____.
7. The doll cost _____ dollars. I think it cost _____ much.
8. It takes _____ to make a quarrel.
9. Do not sing _____ loud.
10. _____ and _____ are four.
11. The sun gives light _____ the moon.
12. I saw _____ bright stars in the sky.

LESSON 17

REPRODUCTION — ORAL

THE LION AND THE FOX

A lion who was old and weak could not go out to hunt for food. He went into his den and made believe that he was very sick.

Many animals went into the den to look at him. When they came near, he caught them and ate them.

After a great many had been caught in this way, a fox came along. He sat down outside the den and asked the lion how he was.

The lion said that he was very sick, and he begged the fox to come in and see him.

"So I would," said the fox, "but I notice that all the footprints point into your den, and that none point out."

LESSON 18

SELECTION TO BE MEMORIZED

LADY MOON

Lady Moon, Lady Moon, where are you roving?
      Over the sea.
Lady Moon, Lady Moon, whom are you loving?
      All that love me.

Are you not tired with rolling, and never
      Resting to sleep?
Why look so pale and so sad, as forever
      Wishing to weep?

Ask me not this, little child, if you love me;
      You are too bold.
I must obey the dear Father above me,
      And do as I'm told.

Lady Moon, Lady Moon, where are you roving?
      Over the sea.
Lady Moon, Lady Moon, whom are you loving?
      All that love me.
                              — LORD HOUGHTON

LESSON 19

WAS — WERE

1. Tom was throwing snowballs.
2. Tom and Frank were throwing snowballs.
3. You were not playing.
4. The children were happy.

How many boys are mentioned in the first sentence?

Is *was* or *were* used in that sentence?

How many boys are mentioned in the second sentence?

Is *was* or *were* used in that sentence?

In which sentence is *you* used?

Is *was* or *were* used with *you?*

In which sentence are a number of children mentioned?

Is *was* or *were* used in that sentence?

Copy these sentences, filling the blanks with *was* or *were*:

1. The day _____ very warm.
2. The boys _____ swimming in the pond.
3. _____ they having a good time?

4. You _____ not at school yesterday.
5. _____ you sick?
6. Two dogs _____ playing in the road.
7. One dog _____ run over by a wagon.
8. Its foot _____ hurt.
9. The children _____ sorry for the poor dog.

LESSON 20

Copy the sentences in Lesson 3, filling the blanks with *was* or *were*.

Fill these blanks with *was* or *were*:

Use _____ in speaking of one.
Use _____ in speaking of more than one.
Use _____ with the word *you*.

Fill the above blanks with *is* or *are*.

LESSON 21

FOR DICTATION AND ORAL REPRODUCTION

Wheat

A farmer planted some wheat.
The sun and rain made the wheat grow.

When the wheat was ripe, the farmer took it to the mill.

The miller ground the wheat and made it into flour.

A grocer bought sacks of flour from the miller.

Mother bought flour from the grocer and made bread and cake for us to eat.

LESSON 22

OBSERVATION LESSON

TREES

Name three kinds of shade trees.

Name eight kinds of fruit trees.

Name five kinds of nut trees.

Name five kinds of trees whose wood is used for lumber.

Name some kinds of trees that grow only in warm countries.

Name some kinds of trees that remain green all winter.

Draw a picture containing three trees.

From a painting by Landseer.

SAVED

LESSON 23

A PICTURE LESSON

Tell what you see in the picture.

How do you suppose the child happened to fall into the water?

Where was the dog?

What did he do?

What is the name of this picture?

What is the name of the artist?

Write a story about this picture.

LESSON 24

A — AN

Copy:

1. Lucy found an egg in a nest in the barn.
2. An eagle builds its nest in the mountains.
3. Hiawatha was an Indian boy.
4. Frank paid two cents for an apple.
5. Have you seen the nest of an oriole?
6. I saw an ugly dog yesterday.

Do the words that follow *an* begin with vowels or with consonants?

LESSON 25

Copy these sentences, filling the blanks with *a* or *an*:

1. _____ owl sat on _____ branch of _____ tree.
2. Tom bought _____ orange and _____ banana.
3. _____ army of men marched up the hill.
4. _____ old man was playing on _____ harp.
5. _____ ape is something like _____ monkey.
6. The girl wanted _____ ice cream soda.
7. Henry saw _____ elephant and _____ tiger.

LESSON 26

DAYS OF THE WEEK

Sunday	Thursday
Monday	Friday
Tuesday	Saturday
Wednesday	

With what kind of letter does the name of each day begin?

Copy these sentences, filling the blanks:

1. There are _____ days in the week.
2. The first day of the week is _____.
3. We go to school on _____, _____, _____, _____, and _____.
4. We play on _____.
5. We go to church on _____.

LESSON 27

COMPOSITION — ORAL OR WRITTEN

When will you have your next vacation? What do you expect to do then?

LESSON 28

SELECTION TO BE MEMORIZED

THE SWING

How do you like to go up in a swing,
   Up in the air so blue?
Oh, I do think it the pleasantest thing
   Ever a child can do!

Up in the air and over the wall,
   Till I can see so wide,
Rivers and trees and cattle and all
   Over the countryside —

Till I look down on the garden green,
   Down on the roof so brown —
Up in the air I go flying again,
   Up in the air and down!
                    — ROBERT LOUIS STEVENSON

How many pictures can you find in this poem?

Draw one of them.

With what kind of letter does the first word of every line of poetry begin?

LESSON 29

WHEN?

Copy these sentences, filling in the blanks with words that answer the question *When?*

1. The violets bloom _____.
2. _____ I eat breakfast.
3. We have dinner _____.
4. _____ we go to church.
5. I like to go to the woods _____.
6. The farmer plants corn _____.
7. The stars shine _____.
8. _____ _____ the sun is in the west.
9. The owl sleeps _____.

LESSON 30

COMPOSITION

What did you do last Saturday morning?
What did you do in the afternoon?

Write your answers in this form:

Last Saturday morning I _____.
In the afternoon I _____.

From a painting by Carter.

AN INTERESTING FAMILY

LESSON 31

ORAL AND WRITTEN

The Rabbit

With what is a rabbit covered?

Describe a rabbit's ears.

What kind of teeth has a rabbit?

Name two other animals that have teeth like a rabbit's.

How does a rabbit sometimes injure trees?

What does a rabbit eat?

Where does a rabbit make its home?

What is the color of the rabbits that live in the fields?

Of what color are most pet rabbits?

Copy these sentences and fill the blanks:

1. A rabbit has _____ fur.
2. It has _____ ears and _____ eyes.
3. It eats _____, _____, and _____.
4. Its teeth are very _____.
5. _____ and _____ have teeth like the rabbit's.
6. Some rabbits are white and some are _____.

LESSON 32

FOR DICTATION

THERE — THEIR

There are some boys playing ball.
Now their ball is lost.
Their dog found it for them.
Don't you want to go over there to play?
Look there! George has fallen down.
The boys are helping their playmate to rise.

LESSON 33

Copy the following sentences, filling the blanks with *there* or *their:*

1. The birds are singing up _____ in the tree.
2. _____ music is sweet.
3. _____ nest is under the eaves.
4. Frank climbed up _____ to see it.
5. _____ were four little birds in the nest.
6. The old birds take good care of _____ little ones.
7. _____ goes the mother bird with a worm in her bill.

Copy from your reader two sentences that contain the word *there*. Copy two that contain

LESSON 34

FOR DICTATION

THE CAT AND THE MICE

Some mice lived in a barn.

A cat lived in the barn, too. She chased the mice. She caught many of them.

One day the mice had a meeting. They talked about the cat. They wished to get rid of her.

LESSON 35

FOR DICTATION

THE CAT AND THE MICE *(CONTINUED)*

One mouse had a plan. It was to tie a bell to the cat's neck. Then the mice would hear the bell and run away.

The mice thought it was a fine plan. They ran to get a bell.

But no mouse wanted to tie the bell on Puss.

LESSON 36

WHERE?

Copy these sentences, filling the blanks with words that answer the question *Where?*

1. _____ stood a large pine tree.
2. _____ were some little boys playing marbles.
3. _____ was a little bird's nest.
4. _____ grew blue violets and yellow buttercups.
5. _____ was a big red automobile that had broken down.
6. _____ was a bush covered with beautiful red roses.
7. _____ were two busy squirrels.
8. _____ came the fire engine.
9. _____ stood the wigwam of Nokomis.
10. _____ were the busy bees.
11. _____ lived a mother rabbit and her little ones.
12. _____ were three little kittens.

LESSON 37

ORAL AND WRITTEN

HAS — HAVE

Copy these sentences:

1. I have a new book.
2. We have new books.
3. Tom has a little sister.
4. You have the wrong answer.
5. They have their fishing rods.
6. The rabbit has long ears.

Fill these blanks with *has* or *have*:

1. _____ you seen the river?
2. Nellie _____ a canary bird.
3. Harry and Nellie _____ roller skates.
4. They _____ ice skates, too.
5. The oriole _____ a nest in that tree.
6. I _____ a drawing pencil.
7. Rover _____ a new collar.
8. _____ you seen it?
9. It _____ his name on it.
10. The horse _____ gone.

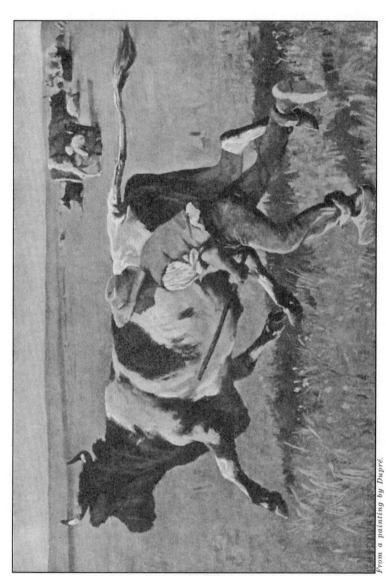

THE ESCAPED COW

From a painting by Dupré.

LESSON 38

A PICTURE LESSON

Tell what you see in the picture.
What time of day do you think it is?
What makes you think so?
What is the boy doing?
What kind of shoes has he?
In what country do they wear such shoes?
What is the woman doing?

What is the name of the picture?
What is the artist's name?

LESSON 39

OBSERVATION LESSON

THE COW

What animal gives us milk?
What forms on top of the milk after it has stood awhile?
Name some things that are made from milk.
Tell how butter is made.
What is the flesh of the cow called?

What use is made of the cow's hide?
What things are made from her horns?
What is made from her hoofs?
What use is made of the hair of the cow?

LESSON 40

COMPOSITION — DESCRIPTION

Read the following questions and directions silently; give the answers as complete sentences.

On what street or road is the school that you attend?
What direction does the building face?
Tell something about the yard. Are there trees in it?
How many rooms are there in the building? Tell something about your room.
How many windows has it? How many pupils can it seat?
Has your room any pictures? Which one do you like best?
Are there any flowers in your schoolroom?

LESSON 41

COMPOSITION

Write sentences telling something about each

dog	rabbit	bluejay
horse	squirrel	oriole
owl	robin	eagle

LESSON 42

THE SEASONS AND MONTHS OF THE YEAR

The seasons are spring, summer, autumn, and winter.

January	July
February	August
March	September
April	October
May	November
June	December

With what kind of letter does the name of each month begin? each season?

FOR DICTATION

The spring months are March, April, and May.

The summer months are June, July, and August.

The autumn months are September, October, and November.

The winter months are December, January, and February.

LESSON 43

WHAT MONTH?

Copy these sentences, filling the blanks with words that answer the question, *What month?*

1. Christmas comes in _____.
2. Washington's birthday is in _____.
3. School begins in _____.
4. Thanksgiving is in _____.
5. New Year's is the first day of _____.
6. _____ is called the "month of roses."
7. Easter usually comes in _____.
8. Decoration Day is in _____.
9. _____ is the shortest month.
10. My birthday is in _____.

LESSON 44

WHAT SEASON?

Copy these sentences, filling the blanks with words that answer the question, *What season?*

1. In _____ the days are short and the nights are long.
2. In _____ the days are long and the nights are short.
3. The farmer sows his corn in the _____.
4. In the _____ the squirrels gather nuts.
5. We skate and make snowballs in _____.
6. The birds go South in the _____; in the _____ they come back to us.

LESSON 45

SEE — SAW — SEEN

1. From my window I can see the river.
2. I saw a boat on the river yesterday.
3. I have seen larger boats on the lake.
4. My brother has seen the ocean.
5. I thought that you had seen the ocean.

What word is used before *seen* in the third sentence on page 33?

What word is used before *seen* in the fourth sentence?

What word is used before *seen* in the fifth sentence?

Copy these sentences, filling the blanks with *see, saw, or seen:*

1. I can _____ the blue sky and the fleecy white clouds.
2. I _____ a rainbow last summer.
3. I have _____ heavy black clouds in the west.
4. Last fall we _____ red and yellow leaves on the maple trees.
5. In the spring we shall _____ wild flowers in the woods.
6. Have you _____ apple trees in blossom?
7. I _____ a little brook in the woods.
8. I have _____ the bees gathering honey.
9. Last summer we _____ a robin's nest in the elm tree.
10. Did you _____ the humming bird among the lilies?

LESSON 46

SELECTION TO BE MEMORIZED

THE BROWN THRUSH

"There's a merry
    brown thrush
    sitting up in the
    tree;
He's singing to me! He's singing to me!"
And what does he say, little girl, little boy?
"Oh, the world's running over with joy!
      Don't you hear? Don't you see?
      Hush! Look! In my tree,
I'm as happy as happy can be!"

And the brown thrush keeps singing, "A nest
    do you see,
And five eggs hid by me in the juniper tree?
Don't meddle! Don't touch! little girl, little
    boy,
Or the world will lose some of its joy!
      Now I'm glad! Now I'm free!
      And I always shall be,
If you never bring sorrow to me."

So the merry brown thrush sings away in the
    tree,
To you and to me, to you and to me;
And he sings all the day, little girl, little
    boy,
"Oh, the world's running over with joy!
       But long it won't be,
        Don't you know? Don't you see?
Unless we are as good as can be."
                      — LUCY LARCOM

Where is the brown thrush?
What is he doing?
Why is he so happy?
Where is his nest?
How many eggs are there
    in the nest?
Copy what the thrush says
    in the last stanza.

LESSON 47

COMPOSITION

Reread the story, "The Dog in the Manger," on page 6; then close your book and write it from memory.

LESSON 48

COMPOSITION

Copy these sentences and fill the blanks with words that answer the question, *How?*

1. The children did their work _____.
2. The dog barked _____.
3. Nellie sews _____.
4. The wind blew _____.
5. The fire horses ran _____.
6. Trees grow _____.
7. The cat purrs _____.
8. The lion roared _____.
9. The bird sings _____.
10. The engineer blew the whistle _____.
11. The man spoke _____ to the child.
12. The mother cat carried her kittens _____ to another home.

LESSON 49
LETTER WRITING

Atlanta, Ga.
Jan. 25, 1910

Dear George,

I hear that you have some rabbits to sell. I want to buy two, if they do not cost too much.

Have you any white ones? How much are they? When may I come to see them?

Let me hear from you soon.

Your friend,
Frank Martin.

Master George Andrews
2116 Maple Ave
Atlanta
Georgia

Copy the letter from Frank to George.

Draw the envelope and copy the address upon it.

What mark of punctuation is placed after *Ave.?* The period indicates that *Ave.* stands for the word Avenue.

The address on an envelope is often written with a comma after each line except the last, where a period is used.

Where should the stamp be placed on an envelope?

LESSON 50

LETTER WRITING

Write George's answer to Frank.
Draw the envelope and direct it to —

Master Frank Martin
1518 South Tenth Street
Atlanta, GA   30341

LESSON 51

DIRECTING ENVELOPES

Draw five envelopes and direct them as follows:

1. To Mr. Ralph Barton, 1407 Grand Ave., Portland, Oregon 97232.
2. To Mrs. S. W. Gray, 320 Main St., Dallas, Texas 75202.
3. To your teacher.
4. To yourself.
5. To a friend who lives in a city in some other state than your own.

LESSON 52

CONVERSATION LESSON

PREPARATION FOR WINTER

How do the plants and trees get ready for winter?
What preparation does the squirrel make?
Name another animal that stores away food.
Where do toads and frogs spend the winter?
What becomes of snakes?
What birds go South?
What change is there in the covering of those that remain?
How do bears spend the winter?
What insects prepare food for winter?
What becomes of the other insects?
What does the caterpillar do?
What difference is there in the coats of horses, dogs, and other animals?

From a painting by Landseer.

SHOEING THE HORSE

LESSON 53

A PICTURE LESSON

What is a man who shoes horses called?
What other work does he do?
What tools does he use?
Tell what you can see in the picture.
Write a story about the picture, telling about the horse's master, where the shoe was lost, why the donkey is in the shop, what the dog's name is, and why he came with the horse. Tell other things that the picture suggests.

Tell the name of another picture which this artist painted.

LESSON 54

FOR DICTATION

Erito is a little Eskimo boy. His home is in Greenland. It is very cold there.

He lives in an igloo. His father made it of blocks of ice.

Erito's clothes are made of skins of animals. He looks like a little bear.

LESSON 55

FOR DICTATION (*Continued*)

There are no horses where Erito lives. His father owns many dogs. These dogs are taught to pull heavy loads.

Erito has two big dogs. He hitches these to his sled, and they draw him over the ice and snow. Many animals live near his home. There are big white bears and seals. There are reindeer, too. Erito hopes to be a hunter some day.

LESSON 56

WHY?

Copy these sentences, filling the blanks with words that answer the question, *Why?*

1. James was late at school because _____.

2. Nellie did not know her lesson because _____.

3. The squirrels had nuts to eat all winter because _____.

4. Tom's garden did not grow because _____.

5. The sun did not shine because _____.

6. I like to go to the woods in summer because _____.

7. Minnie did not go to the picnic because _____.

8. The boys like to play with Frank because _____.

9. They do not like to play with Arthur because _____.

10. The boy was praying because _____.

LESSON 57

SELECTION TO BE MEMORIZED

DUTCH LULLABY

Wynken, Blynken, and Nod one night
　　Sailed off in a wooden shoe—
Sailed on a river of crystal light
　　Into a sea of dew.
"Where are you going, and what do you wish?"
　　The old moon asked the three.
"We have come to fish for the herring fish
　　That live in this beautiful sea;
　　Nets of silver and gold have we,"
　　　　　　Said Wynken,
　　　　　　Blynken,
　　　　　　And Nod.

The old moon laughed and sang a song,
　　As they rocked in the wooden shoe;
And the wind that sped them all night long
　　Ruffled the waves of dew;
The little stars were the herring fish
　　That lived in that beautiful sea.
"Now cast your nets wherever you wish,

But never afeard are we!"
So cried the stars to the fishermen three:
>Wynken,
>Blynken,
>And Nod.

All night long their nets they threw
To the stars in the twinkling foam;
Then down from the sky came the wooden shoe
Bringing the fishermen home;
'Twas all so pretty a sail, it seemed
As if it could not be;
And some folks thought 'twas a dream they'd
dreamed
Of sailing that beautiful sea;
But I shall name you the fishermen three:
>Wynken,
>Blynken,
>And Nod.

Wynken and Blynken are two little eyes,
And Nod is a little head,
And the wooden shoe that sailed the skies
Is a wee one's trundle-bed;

So shut your eyes while mother sings
   Of wonderful sights that be,
And you shall see the beautiful things
   As you rock in the misty sea,
   Where the old shoe rocked the fishermen
     three:
          Wynken,
          Blynken,
          And Nod.

            — EUGENE FIELD

LESSON 58

THE COMMA

A horse can run and trot and gallop and walk.

A horse can run, trot, gallop, and walk.

How many times is *and* used in the first sentence?

How many times is *and* used in the second sentence?

Where are commas used in the second sentence?

Do not use *and* more than once in any one sentence of the following:

1. Write a sentence telling three things that a bird can do.

2. Write a sentence telling four things that a cat can do.

3. Write a sentence telling three things that a baby can do.

4. Write a sentence telling three things that a carpenter can do.

LESSON 59

OBSERVATION LESSON

SEEDS

What seeds are scattered by the wind?

What seeds are scattered by clinging to the fur of animals and to the clothing of people?

What seeds are carried by birds?

What seeds have shells?

What seeds grow in pods?

What seeds have husks around them?

What seeds have pulp around them?

LESSON 60

REPRODUCTION — ORAL AND WRITTEN

THE GREEDY DOG

A dog was once carrying home a fine piece of meat. On his way he had to cross a bridge.

He looked down and saw his reflection in the water.

He thought it was another dog with a larger piece of meat. He dropped his piece and jumped into the water to get the other piece of meat.

But there was no other dog. His meat fell to the bottom, where he could not get it, and he had to go without his dinner.

This is a good story for greedy people.

Rewrite this story in your own words.

LESSON 61

CAPITALS

Copy:

Chicago	Texas	Abraham Lincoln
New York	Kansas	George Washington

With what kind of letter does the name of a person or place begin?

1. Write your father's name.

2. Write the name of your teacher.

3. Write the names of three girls.

4. Write the names of three boys.

5. Write the name of the state in which you live.

6. Write the name of the governor of your state.

7. Write the name of the capital of your state.

8. Write the name of the largest city in your state.

9. Write the name of the President of the United States.

10. Write the name of the capital of the United States.

11. Write the name of the largest city in the United States.

LESSON 62

OBSERVATION LESSON — MATERIALS

Chairs and tables are made of _____.

Railroad tracks are made of _____.

Shoes are made of _____.

Calico is made of _____.

Linen is made of _____.

Some buildings are made of _____, and some are made of _____.

Bricks are made of _____.

Some money is made of _____, and some is made of _____.

Needles are made of _____.

Paper is made of _____.

Warm clothes are made of _____.

Glass is made of _____.

Some candles are made of _____, and some are made of _____.

Horseshoes are made of _____.

Nails are made of _____.

Copy eight of the above sentences and fill the blanks.

LESSON 63

INITIALS

Henry Wadsworth Longfellow
Henry W. Longfellow
H. W. Longfellow
H. W. L.

The first letter of a word is its *initial* letter.

What is the initial letter of Henry? of Wadsworth? of Longfellow?

Initial letters of a name are called *initials*.

What mark of punctuation follows an initial when used alone?
With what kind of letter is an initial

Copy these names, using the initial instead of the middle name:

Ralph Waldo Emerson
John Greenleaf Whittier
Edwin Henry Landseer
William Makepeace Thackeray

Copy these names, using the initial instead of the first name:

Theodore Roosevelt   Walter Scott
Charles Dickens   Daniel Webster

Copy these names, using the initials instead of the first and middle names:

Edgar Allan Poe   Henry Ward Beecher
Julia Ward Howe   Ulysses Simpson Grant

LESSON 64

SELECTION TO BE READ AND STUDIED

THE JOURNEY

I never saw the hills so far
And blue, the way the pictures are;

And flowers, flowers growing thick,
And not a one for me to pick!

The land was running from the train
All blurry from the windowpane;

And then it all looked flat and still,
When up there jumped a little hill!

I saw the windows and the spires,
And sparrows sitting on the wires;

And fences running up and down;
And then we cut straight through a town.

I saw a valley, like a cup;
And ponds that twinkled and dried up.

I counted meadows that were burnt;
And there were trees, and then there weren't!

We crossed the bridges with a roar,
Then hummed the way we went before.

And tunnels made it dark and light
Like openwork of day or night;

Until I saw the chimneys rise,
And lights and lights and lights, like eyes.

And when they took me through the door,
I heard it all begin to roar—

I thought, as far as I could see,
That everybody wanted me!

— JOSEPHINE PRESTON PEABODY

Did you ever journey on a train?

Where did you go?

What things did you see from the window?

Did you see anything that is spoken of in this poem?

How many pictures can you find?

Draw two of them.

LESSON 65

OBSERVATION LESSON

WHAT COLOR?

Copy these sentences, filling the blanks with words that answer the question, *Of what color?*

1. Grass is _____.   5. Coal is _____.
2. Gold is _____.   6. Bananas are _____.
3. Salt is _____.   7. Wild roses are _____.
4. The sky is _____. 8. Cherries are _____.

9. In autumn the maple leaves are _____ and _____.

10. A watermelon is _____ on the outside and _____ on the inside.

11. A woodpecker has a _____ head.

12. Daisies are _____ and _____.
13. Some grapes are _____, and some are _____.

LESSON 66
LETTER WRITING

Copy this letter:

Detroit, Mich.
May 10, 1911

Dear Bessie,

I found out that to-morrow is your birthday, and I am sending you a box of letter paper for a present.

I hope you will have many happy birthdays.

Your friend,
Lillian Edwards.

LESSON 67

LETTER WRITING

Write Bessie's answer to Lillian's letter, thanking her for the present and telling what other presents she received.

Draw the envelope and direct it. Lillian lives at 2632 Walnut St., Detroit, Michigan 33625.

LESSON 68

SELECTION TO BE MEMORIZED

My Shadow

I have a little shadow that goes in and out
    with me,
And what can be the use of him is more than
    I can see.
He is very, very like me from heels up to
    the head;
And I see him jump before me, when I jump
    into my bed.

The funniest thing about him is the way he
    likes to grow —

Not at all like proper children, which is always
    very slow;
For he sometimes shoots up taller, like an India-
    rubber ball,
And he sometimes gets so little that there's none
    of him at all.

He hasn't got a notion of how children ought to
    play,
And can only make a fool of me in every sort of
    way.
He stays so close beside me, he's a coward you
    can see;
I'd think shame to stick to nanny as that shadow
    sticks to me!

One morning, very early, before the sun was up,
I rose and found the shining dew on every
    buttercup;
But my lazy little shadow, like an arrant
    sleepyhead,
Had stayed at home behind me and was fast
    asleep in bed.

— Robert Louis Stevenson

LESSON 69

REPRODUCTION — ORAL

THE WIND AND THE SUN

One day the wind and the sun had a quarrel. Each thought he was stronger than the other. While they were talking, a man came in sight. They agreed that the one who could make the man take off his coat was the stronger.

The wind tried first. He blew and blew, but the man only held his coat closer about him. The wind tried again, but it was of no use. The wind had to give up.

Then the sun came out from behind a cloud. He sent some of his warmest rays down on the man's head. The man became very warm. He unbuttoned his coat. He became still warmer, and at last he took his coat off and carried it on his arm.

The wind agreed that the sun was the stronger.

Write the first paragraph from dictation.

LESSON 70

ABBREVIATIONS

Jan. — January	Sun. — Sunday
Feb. — February	Mon. — Monday
Mar. — March	Tues. — Tuesday
Apr. — April	Wed. — Wednesday
Aug. — August	Thurs. — Thursday
Sept. — September	Fri. — Friday
Oct. — October	Sat. — Saturday
Nov. — November	Mr. — Mister
Dec. — December	Dr. — Doctor
St. — Street	
Ave. — Avenue	

In writing, words are sometimes shortened, or abbreviated.

What mark of punctuation follows each abbreviation?

What is the abbreviation of the name of the state in which you live?

Name another state. What is the abbreviation?

Copy the above list.

Write the list from dictation.

LIONS AT HOME

From a painting by Rosa Bonheur.

LESSON 71

A PICTURE STORY

How many lions can you see in the picture?
Which is the father lion?
Which is the mother lion?
What do the little ones remind you of?
What is the artist's name?

LESSON 72

FOR DICTATION

I am a lion. I live far away in Africa. In many ways I am like a cat. I have sharp teeth and sharp claws. I have cushions on my feet so that I can walk softly. I can see as well at night as in the daytime.

I hunt for my prey and spring upon it.

I am called the "King of Beasts."

LESSON 73

COMPOSITION

Write a story that a horse might tell about himself, if he could talk.

LESSON 74
COMPOSITION

Write a story in which you use these

Bessie Thomas	woods	bluebird
violets	lunch	Saturday
basket	squirrel	afternoon

Write a story in which you use these

Frank Wilson	owner	five dollars
pocketbook	reward	found

LESSON 75
DATES

January 16, 1840
December 25, 1775
August 6, 1909
November 30, 1899
March 13, 1776

September 19, 1900
February 14, 1910
October 31, 1900
April 22, 1770
December 1, 1645

What mark of punctuation is placed between the day of the month and the year?

Write these dates from dictation, using the abbreviation for the name of the month.

LESSON 76

OBSERVATION LESSON

Name four parts of a chair.

Name five parts of a watch.

Name as many parts as you can of a street car.

Name several parts of a wagon.

Name five parts of a clock.

Name four or more parts of a sewing machine.

Name four parts of a harness.

Name as many parts as you can of an automobile.

Name six parts of a house.

LESSON 77

EAT — ATE — EATEN

1. When did you eat your breakfast?

2. I ate it this morning.

3. I have eaten my lunch and must go to school.

4. Tom has eaten his lunch, too.

5. Nellie had eaten an apple before I came home.

What word is used before *eaten* in the third sentence on page 65?

What word is used before *eaten* in the fourth sentence?

What word is used before *eaten* in the fifth sentence?

Copy these sentences, filling the blanks with *eat*, *ate*, or *eaten*:

1. Why don't you _____ more?
2. I _____ a lunch before dinner, and I am not hungry.
3. I have _____ a peach and a banana.
4. What did the boy _____ that made him sick?
5. He _____ some green apples.
6. Have you _____ your lunch?
7. I _____ it an hour ago.
8. Did you _____ it at school?
9. I _____ it in the yard under the trees.
10. I have _____ it there every day this fall.
11. In winter the squirrels _____ the nuts that they had gathered in summer.
12. After they had _____ their dinner, they slept.

LESSON 78

SELECTION TO BE MEMORIZED

ONE, TWO, THREE

It was an old, old, old, old lady,
And a boy that was half-past three;
And the way that they played together
Was beautiful to see.

She couldn't go romping and jumping,
And the boy, no more could he;
For he was a thin little fellow,
With a thin little twisted knee.

They sat in the yellow sunlight,
Out under the maple tree;
And the game that they played I'll tell you
Just as it was told to me.

It was Hide-and-Go-Seek they were playing,
Though you'd never have known it to be —
With an old, old, old, old lady,
And a boy with a twisted knee.

The boy would bend his face down
  On his one little sound right knee,
And he'd guess where she was hiding,
  In guesses One, Two, Three.

"You are in the china closet!"
  He would cry, and laugh with glee —
It wasn't the china closet,
  But he still had Two and Three.

"You are up in papa's big bedroom,
  In the chest with the queer old key!"
And she said, "You are warm and warmer,
  But you're not quite right," said she.

"It can't be the little cupboard
  Where mamma's things used to be —
So it must be the clothespress, Gran'ma!"
  And he found her with his Three.

Then she covered her face with her fingers
  That were wrinkled and white and wee,
And she guessed where the boy was hiding,
  With a One and a Two and a Three.

And they never had stirred from their places,
 Right under the maple tree —
This old, old, old, old lady,
 And the boy with the lame little knee —
This dear, dear, dear old lady,
 And the boy who was half-past three.

— HENRY CUYLER BUNNER

LESSON 79

FOR DICTATION

THE WIND

The wind blows the clouds.
It sails the ships upon the seas.
It dries the clothes on the line.
It makes the windmills pump water.
It scatters seeds.
It blows away dust and bad air.

LESSON 80

ONE AND MORE THAN ONE

Write these words so that they will mean more than one:

apple	lion	boy	doll
girl	clock	rabbit	hat
squirrel	car	book	basket
chair	pencil	cow	bird
flower	tree	sister	brother

What letter did you add to each of these words to make it mean more than one?

LESSON 81

REPRODUCTION — ORAL AND WRITTEN

The Fox and the Crow

A crow stole a piece of cheese and flew with it to a tree. A hungry fox came by. He saw the cheese and wanted it. He wondered how he could get it. He began to talk to the crow.

"What a beautiful bird you are!" he said. "What glossy feathers you have!"

The crow liked to hear this, so she sat still and listened.

"I know," continued the fox, "that you must have a sweet voice. How I wish I could hear you sing!"

The crow was so pleased that she opened her mouth to sing. The cheese fell to the ground. The fox quickly picked it up and ran off with it.

Draw a picture suggested by this story.

LESSON 82

ONE AND MORE THAN ONE

glass	glasses
box	boxes

Sometimes we add *es* to a word to make it mean more than one.

Copy these words, writing them so that they will mean more than one:

fox	church	match	peach	dish
dress	brush	bench	bush	watch

LESSON 83

REPRODUCTION — ORAL AND WRITTEN

Silk

A pretty white moth laid some eggs on the leaves of a mulberry tree.

Little worms came from the eggs.

They were hungry, and they ate the green leaves.

After a while they grew sleepy.

They spun soft, silken covers around themselves and went to sleep.

While they were sleeping, some men came and carried them away.

The soft threads of silk were carefully unrolled.

Machines made the thread into beautiful silk cloth.

A big ship carried this cloth far across the sea.

A rich merchant bought the cloth and placed it in his shop.

One day a lady saw it there. "What a beautiful piece of silk!" she said. "I will buy it and make a dress for my little girl."

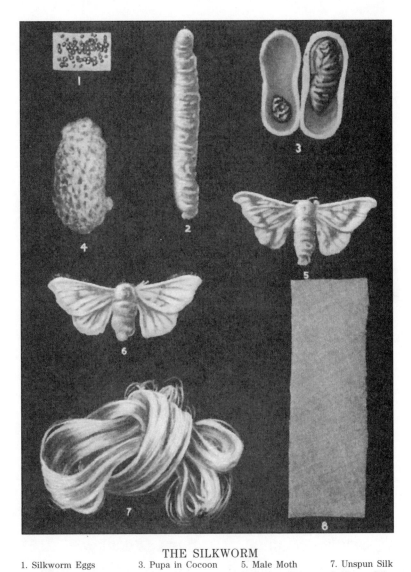

THE SILKWORM

1. Silkworm Eggs	3. Pupa in Cocoon	5. Male Moth	7. Unspun Silk
2. Fourth Stage Worm	4. Cocoon	6. Female Moth	8. Woven Silk

LESSON 84

LETTER WRITING

Portland, Oregon

April 22, 1910

Dear Henry,

Did you lose a knife at the picnic, Saturday? I found one, which Carl Turner thought was like the one you received last Christmas. Did your knife have two blades?

Your friend,

Albert Burton.

Write Henry's answer to Albert's letter, describing the knife and stating where he thought he lost it.

LESSON 85

ONE AND MORE THAN ONE

Copy these words, writing in one column the words that mean *one*, and in another column the words that mean *more than one:*

ladies	mice	foot	donkey
pony	berries	feet	mouse

lady	knives	fly	cherry
men	goose	teeth	turkeys
piano	oxen	women	child
knife	lilies	geese	ox
ponies	children	man	woman

From your reader copy ten words that mean *one*, and ten that mean *more than one*.

LESSON 86

READING LESSON — DIALOGUE FOR TWO

1. Who is it? It is I.
2. Did you knock at the door? No, it was not I; it was he.
3. Is that your brother? Yes, it is he.
4. Who called? It was I.
5. Who threw the snowballs? It was they.
6. Did Mary speak? I think it was she.
7. Who fell down? It was not I.
8. Who laughed? It was we.
9. Who was standing at the window? It was she.

10. Did Helen break her doll? No, it was I who broke it.

11. Is your cousin here? Yes, that is he.

NOTE TO THE TEACHER. — This lesson should be repeated in many different recitations, until the forms no longer seem strange or unusual.

LESSON 87

CHOICE OF WORDS

Choose words from the list below to fill blanks in the following sentences:

1. The book is _____ the table.
2. The pencil is on the floor _____ the table.
3. Nellie lives _____ the street.
4. Is your mother _____ home?
5. I think she has gone _____ the concert.
6. We threw sticks _____ the water, and Rover went after them.
7. Is Frank _____ the house?
8. The blue sky is _____ us.
9. The air is _____ us.

on	to	by	above	around	into
at	in	for	under	across	after

LESSON 88

WHOSE?

1. The desk belonging to the teacher is at the front of the room.
2. The teacher's desk is at the front of the room.
3. The nest of the little bird is at the top of the tree.
4. The little bird's nest is at the top of the tree.

Is there any difference in the meaning between the first and second sentences?

What does 's added to the word *teacher* show?

Is there any difference in the meaning between the third and fourth sentences?

What does 's added to the word *bird* show?

Write these sentences from dictation:

1. Nellie's new dress was torn.
2. The dog's master went away on the train.
3. Tom's book has beautiful pictures in it.
4. Mr. White's horse ran away.
5. Did you see Frank's little pony?

LESSON 89

Copy these sentences and fill the blanks with words that answer the question, *Whose?*

1. The _____ playthings were on the floor.
2. The poor _____ coat was ragged.
3. Uncle _____ farm is near the city.
4. A _____ bite is poisonous.
5. _____ skates were bright and new.
6. The _____ light is very bright.
7. The lazy _____ work was not finished.
8. _____ father is sick.
9. The _____ song is sweet.
10. The fox stole the _____ cheese.
11. The _____ little ones are called kids.
12. The _____ little ones are called kittens.
13. The _____ little ones are called puppies.

LESSON 90

Use these words in sentences:

Harry's	dog's	father's
Edith's	horse's	children's
Mr. Smith's	rabbit's	squirrel's

LESSON 91

SELECTION TO BE MEMORIZED

THE WONDERFUL WORLD

Great, wide, wonderful, beautiful World,
With the wonderful water above you curled,
And the wonderful grass upon your breast —
World, you are beautifully dressed!

The wonderful air is over me,
And the wonderful wind is shaking the tree;
It walks on the water and whirls the mills,
And talks to itself on the tops of the hills.

You friendly Earth, how far do you go,
With wheat fields that nod, and rivers that flow.
With cities and gardens, and oceans and isles,
And people upon you for thousands of miles?

Ah, you are so great and I am so small,
I hardly can think of you, World, at all;
And yet, when I said my prayers today,
My mother kissed me, and said, quite gay:

"If the wonderful World is great to you,
And great to father and mother, too,
You are more than the Earth, though you are
  such a dot!
You can love and think, and the Earth cannot!"

— William Brighty Rands

LESSON 92

GO — WENT— GONE

1. I go to school every day.
2. I went to the country last summer.
3. Mother has gone to Chicago.
4. The girls have gone home.
5. I called for you this morning, but you had gone.
6. I think that all the children have gone.

What word is used before *gone* in the third sentence?
What word is used before *gone* in the fourth sentence?
What word is used before *gone* in the fifth sentence? In the sixth sentence?

Copy these sentences and fill the blanks with *go*, *went*, or *gone*:

1. We _____ to school five days in the week.
2. Fred _____ to the country last summer.
3. The birds have _____ to the warm South land.
4. When spring comes, the snow will _____ away.
5. Nellie's big brother has _____ away to school.
6. The children _____ to the park last summer.
7. The boys have _____ across the street to play ball.
8. The girls took their dolls and _____ down by the river.
9. Rover has _____ with Frank after the cows.
10. The birds will return when the snow has _____ away.
11. Wynken, Blynken, and Nod _____ off in a wooden shoe.
12. They had not _____ far when they saw the moon.

LESSON 93

REPRODUCTION — ORAL

THE LION AND THE MOUSE

A lion was sleeping in his den when a little mouse ran across his face and woke him up. He put out his paw and caught the mouse. He was about to kill the little creature, but the mouse begged so hard for her life that the lion let her go.

Some time after, the lion was caught in a net that the hunters had set. He roared and struggled, but the net was too strong for him to break. The mouse heard him roaring and ran to help him. She nibbled through the cords that held him, and the lion was again free. He was glad that he had saved the life of the little mouse.

LESSON 94

Copy what the lion says and supply what the mouse says:

Lion. Something woke me up. I wonder what

it was. Here is something under my paw. Why, it is a mouse! Why did you wake me up?

Mouse. _____ _____ _____.

Lion. I am going to eat you.
Mouse. _____ _____ _____.

Lion. Why should I let you go?
Mouse. _____ _____ _____.

Lion. I will let you go this time, but don't wake me again.

LESSON 95

CONVERSATION LESSON

For breakfast, a boy had oatmeal with cream and sugar, a piece of beefsteak, which was seasoned with pepper and salt, some buttered toast, and a cup of cocoa.

Tell something about each article of food, where it was obtained, and who had to work before it was ready to be eaten.

LESSON 96

CONTRACTIONS

doesn't	they'll
I'm	haven't
aren't	can't
isn't	o'clock
weren't	didn't
couldn't	shouldn't
wouldn't	don't
we'll	they're
hasn't	it's

Of what two words is each of the above words composed?   What mark shows that a letter or letters have been omitted?

Copy the list, writing after each word its equivalent.

LESSON 97

In column 2 on the next page, find a word opposite in meaning to each word in column 1. Copy the words in pairs; thus, *hot — cold.*

1	2
black	difficult
hot	bad
slow	low
hard	ugly
sour	dry
narrow	soft
short	cold
dark	fast
late	white
straight	poor
wet	noisy
beautiful	big
high	rough
good	wide
smooth	sweet
well	old
little	long
new	tall
rich	crooked
easy	light
quiet	sick
thick	early
short	thin

LESSON 98

Use in sentences the first ten words of column 1 on page 85.

LESSON 99

COMPOSITION

What is your name?

How old are you?

Where do you live?

Have you brothers and sisters? If so, tell their names.

Where do you go to school?

How long have you been going to school?

What grade are you in?

How many pupils are there in your class?

What study do you like best?

What do you play after school and on Saturdays?

What games do you like best?

What work can you do?

Write answers to the above questions.

LESSON 100

REPRODUCTION

THE HUMMING BIRD AND THE BUTTERFLY

Humming Bird. What a beautiful creature you are! What splendid wings you have! Do come with me and be my friend.

Butterfly. No, thank you, Mrs. Humming Bird, I cannot be your friend.

Humming Bird. Why not?

Butterfly. You once made fun of me and said that I was ugly and stupid.

Humming Bird. That is impossible. I am sure I never called you stupid or ugly.

Butterfly. You may not call me that now, but when you made fun of me I was a caterpillar. You did not know that I would some day be a butterfly. You see it is best to be kind to everybody, for ugly creatures sometimes become beautiful. So good-bye; I prefer to find other friends.

Tell what you know of the change of a caterpillar to a butterfly.

LESSON 101

Write an account of a conversation between a rabbit and a squirrel. Use the same form as that given in Lesson 100.

LESSON 102

A PICTURE LESSON

What do you see in the picture?

How does a mother show that she loves her baby?

Does a cow love her calf? How does she show it?

How does a cat show her love for her kittens?

What will a mother dog do if her puppies are hurt?

What other animals have you seen that showed love for their young ones?

How does a mother bird care for her little ones?

What is the name of the picture?

Write a story about the picture.

From a painting by Debat-Ponsan.

TWO MOTHERS

LESSON 103

OBSERVATION LESSON

TOOLS

What tools does a carpenter use?
What tools does a blacksmith use?
What tools does a shoemaker use?
What tools does a stone mason use?
What tools and machinery does a farmer use?
What tools does a dentist use?
What tools does a woman use in cooking?
What tools do you use in your work at school?

LESSON 104

SELECTION TO BE MEMORIZED

NOVEMBER

The leaves are fading and falling,
The winds are rough and wild,
The birds have ceased their calling,
But let me tell you, my child,

Though day by day, as it closes,
　　Doth darker and colder grow,
The roots of the bright red roses
　　Will keep alive in the snow.

And when the winter is over,
　　The boughs will get new leaves,
The quail will come back to the clover,
　　And the swallow back to the eaves.

The robin will wear on his bosom
　　A vest that is bright and new,
And the loveliest wayside blossoms
　　Will shine with the sun and dew.

The leaves today are whirling,
　　The brooks are all dry and dumb,
But let me tell you, my darling,
　　The spring will be sure to come.

There must be rough, cold weather,
　　And winds and rains so wild;
Not all good things together
　　Come to us here, my child.

So, when some dear joy loses
   Its beauteous summer glow,
Think how the roots of the roses
   Are kept alive in the snow.

— ALICE CARY

The parts into which this poem is divided are called *stanzas*.

How many stanzas are there in this poem?
With what kind of letter does each line begin?
Copy the first stanza.
Copy two words that describe roses.
Copy two words that describe blossoms.
Copy one word that describes leaves.
Copy two words that describe the wind.
Copy two words that describe weather.
Who wrote this poem?

LESSON 105

Fill these blanks with words from the list at the end of the lesson.

1. An owl cannot _____.
2. We _____ in school yesterday.

3. The teacher _____ the bell at nine o'clock.
4. The goldenrod _____ in the woods last fall.
5. We have _____ that song many times.
6. Did you hear me _____ the bell?
7. I have _____ it many times.
8. How tall that tree has _____!
9. I _____ you would come.
10. Do you _____ your lesson?
11. I have _____ you a long time.

sing	ring	know	grow
sang	rang	knew	grew
sung	rung	known	grown

LESSON 106

REPRODUCTION — ORAL AND WRITTEN

An Acorn

Many years ago an acorn fell by the side of a little river.

It grew and grew until it was larger than any tree near it.

One day men came with their axes and cut it down.

It floated down the river with other logs.

After it had gone many miles, men caught it with hooks and drew it into a sawmill.

Large saws cut it into lumber.

A train carried the lumber far away to a city.

Here it was taken from the train, put into wagons, and carried to a vacant lot.

Carpenters then cut the lumber into lengths for the floor of a fine house.

Read this story, close your books, and write the story from memory.

Draw a picture suggested by this lesson.

LESSON 107

MOST — ALMOST

1. It is <u>almost</u> five o'clock.
2. Which boy has the <u>most</u> money?
3. I think Frank has the <u>most</u>.
4. My work is <u>almost</u> done.

In which of the above sentences can *nearly* be used instead of the underlined word?

Copy these sentences and fill the blanks with *almost* or *most*:

1. Harry is _____ as tall as Charles.
2. _____ of the birds go south in winter.
3. The lion _____ caught the deer.
4. Nellie is _____ nine years old.
5. _____ children like to play.
6. The man _____ missed the train.
7. _____ trees shed their leaves in the fall.

Copy from your readers two sentences that contain the word *almost*. Copy two sentences that contain the word *most*.

LESSON 108

OBSERVATION LESSON

What direction is opposite south?
What direction is opposite west?
What direction is opposite north?
What direction is opposite east?
What direction is between north and east?
What direction is between north and west?
What direction is between south and east?

What direction is between south and west?

Where does the sun rise?

Where does the sun set?

In what direction is your home from the schoolhouse?

Mention something that is north of the schoolhouse.

Mention something that is west of your home.

LESSON 109

FOR DICTATION

INSECTS

An insect has six legs. The body of an insect is divided into three parts. On its head are two long feelers, called antennae. Many insects have two or four wings.

Some insects live in the air, some make their homes in the earth, and some live in the water.

Name six insects.

Write sentences, telling something about each of the six insects.

LESSON 110

REPRODUCTION — ORAL

THE FOX AND THE GRAPES

One day a fox saw some grapes at the top of a high grapevine. He was thirsty, and he thought how good the juicy grapes would taste.

He jumped and tried to reach them, but he could not. He tried again and again, but in vain.

At last he said: "I don't care; I don't want

Into how many *parts* is this story divided?
What does the first part tell about?
What does the second part tell about?
What does the third part tell about?

Each of these parts is a *paragraph*.
How many paragraphs are there in the story?
What shows the beginning of a paragraph?

Write the first two paragraphs of this story from dictation.
Draw a picture suggested by this story.

From a painting by Paton.

"YOU'RE NO CHICKEN"

LESSON 111

A PICTURE LESSON

What do you see in the picture?
Tell what you know about frogs.

Write a conversation between the chickens
and the frog, using the following form:

Chicken. _____.
Frog. _____.
Chicken. _____.
Frog. _____.

Let the chickens ask the questions and the frog reply, telling things about himself.

LESSON 112

OBSERVATION LESSON — ORAL

SPIDERS

How many legs has a spider?

How many legs has a fly? An ant? A bee?

Into how many parts is the body of the spider divided?

Into how many parts are the bodies of the ant and the bee divided?

What does the spider spin?

What is the purpose of spinning the web?

When a fly or other insect is caught in the web, what does the spider do?

Where does the spider place its eggs?

Read the questions silently; answer in complete statements.

Draw a spider's web, showing the spider in the center of it.

LESSON 113

CONVERSATION AND REPRODUCTION

THE OSTRICH

The ostrich is the largest of all birds.

It lives in the hot, sandy deserts of Africa.

Ostriches sometimes live in herds with zebras and giraffes.

The nest of the ostrich is made in the sand. About thirty eggs are laid in the nest, and a number are laid outside. Those outside are broken to feed the young ones that are hatched in the nest. One of the parent birds sits on the nest at night, and the sun keeps the eggs warm in the daytime.

Write a short composition, telling all you can about ostriches.

LESSON 114

SELECTION TO BE MEMORIZED

He prayeth best who loveth best
   All things both great and small;
For the dear God who loveth us,
   He made and loveth all.

— SAMUEL TAYLOR COLERIDGE

Write the above quotation from memory.

LESSON 115

REPRODUCTION — ORAL AND WRITTEN

MOTH AND BUTTERFLY

The antennae of a butterfly have little knobs, or balls, on the ends. The antennae of a moth are sometimes like little feathers; they never have knobs on them.

When resting a butterfly holds its wings erect. A moth, when resting, spreads its wings flat over its back.

A butterfly flies in the daytime. A moth usually flies at night.

The body of a moth is heavier than that of a butterfly.

Into how many paragraphs is this selection divided?

What does each paragraph tell about?

Write this selection from memory, using the same number of paragraphs.

LESSON 116

LETTER WRITING

Detroit, Michigan
May 23, 1911

Dear Helen,

I am sick today and cannot go to the library. Won't you please get a book for me? I am eager to read "Black Beauty." If you cannot get that, send me some other book about animals.

Your friend,
Ethel Davis.

Copy the above letter.
Write the letter from dictation.

LESSON 117

LETTER WRITING

Write Helen's answer to Ethel's letter, stating that she could not get "Black Beauty," but is sending her another book. Tell the name of the book and something about it. Helen hopes that Ethel will soon be well.

LESSON 118

EXCLAMATION POINT

Read the first stanza of "The Swing" in Lesson 28. The mark after the fourth line is an *exclamation point.*

How many other exclamation points can you find in the poem?

Read the poem, "The Brown Thrush," Lesson 46. Copy the parts that are followed by exclamation points.

Find ten exclamation points in your reader. Copy the words or sentences that are followed by these points.

LESSON 119

SELECTION TO BE MEMORIZED

THE BLUEBIRD

I know the song that the bluebird is singing,
Out in the apple tree where he is swinging.
Brave little fellow! the skies may be dreary,—
Nothing cares he while his heart is so cheery.

Hark! how the music leaps out from his throat!
Hark! was there ever so merry a note?
Listen a while, and you'll hear what he's saying,
Up in the apple tree, swinging and swaying.

"Dear little blossoms down under the snow,
You must be weary of winter, I know;
Hark while I sing you a message of cheer;
Summer is coming, and springtime is here."

"Little white snowdrop! I pray you arise;
Bright yellow crocus, come, open your eyes.
Sweet little violets, hid from the cold,
Put on your mantles of purple and gold.
Daffodils! Daffodils! say, do you hear?
Summer is coming, and springtime is here."

— EMILY HUNTINGTON MILLER

LESSON 120

COMPOSITION

A robin has been down South all winter; he has just returned to some place near your home. He and his mate are looking for a place to build a nest.

Write a story that the robin might tell if he could talk. Begin your story in this way:

A ROBIN'S STORY

I have just returned from the South. I am a little tired from flying so far, but I am glad to be back again.

LESSON 121

QUOTATIONS AND QUOTATION MARKS

"I wish we could have some fun this afternoon," said Harry.

"Let us go to the pond and fish," said Will.

"We must ask mother if we may," said Harry.

Mother said, "Yes, you may go, and here is something nice for your lunch."

What are the exact words that Will said? Repeat the exact words of the mother.

When the *exact words of another* are repeated, these words are called a *direct quotation.*
The marks (" "), that inclose a direct quotation are called *quotation marks.*
What other mark of punctuation is placed after the direct quotation in the first sentence?   In the second sentence?   In the third sentence?
Where are commas used in the fourth sentence?

Write the above conversation from dictation.

LESSON 122

FOR DICTATION

The Hare and the Tortoise

"What a slow fellow you are!" said a hare to a tortoise. "I feel sorry for anyone who has to creep along as you do."

"Slow as I am, I can beat you," replied the tortoise.

"You think you can beat me, do you?" said the hare. "Let us race to that big tree."

LESSON 123

FOR DICTATION

THE HARE AND THE TORTOISE *(Continued)*

The tortoise started at once and kept straight on. The hare went a little way and then lay down and took a nap. By and by he awoke and ran as fast as he could.

But when he reached the big tree the tortoise was there waiting for him.

"Slow and steady wins the race," said the tortoise.

LESSON 124

REPRODUCTION — ORAL AND WRITTEN

AN INDIAN MYTH — THE ORIGIN OF THE BIRDS

The Indians tell many interesting myths about the birds. They say that many years ago, before there were any birds, the Indian god touched the earth wherever he wished a tree to appear, and trees immediately sprang up.

When the first summer passed and autumn came, the leaves turned red and yellow and brown, just as they do now.

The wind blew and they fluttered through the air and fell to the ground.

The Indian god loved them so much that he did not wish them to die, but to live and be beautiful always. So he changed each bright leaf into a bird and gave it wings and strength with which to fly.

From the red-brown oak, the robin came. The red maple leaves became cardinal birds, the yellow willow leaves were changed to yellow birds, and the brown leaves on other trees became sparrows and larks.

The Indians say that this is why the birds love the trees and live among them, and find food and shelter in their branches and leaves.

—Adapted from "THE PLAN BOOK," by permission of the Publishers, A. FLANAGAN COMPANY.

109

LESSON 125

SELECTION FOR STUDY

Who Made the Stars?

"Mother, who made the stars which light
The beautiful blue sky?
Who made the moon, so clear and bright,
That rises up so high?"

"'Twas God, my child, the Glorious One.
He formed them by His power;
He made alike the brilliant sun,
And every leaf and flower."

"In all the changing scenes of time,
On Him our hopes depend;
In every age, in every clime,
Our Father and our Friend."

— Selected

How many words in this poem refer to God?
With what kind of letter does each of these
words begin?
How many stanzas are there in this poem?
Which lines in each stanza are indented?

From a painting by Elizabeth Gardner.

SOAP BUBBLES

LESSON 126

A PICTURE LESSON

What do you see in the picture?
What are the children doing?
Tell how to make soap bubbles.
Write a story about the picture, telling the names of the children, who the oldest girl is, how old the younger ones are, and what grade they are in at school. Tell what time of year it is. Add other items to your story.

LESSON 127

WOOL

On a warm day in April, Farmer Bailey went out to look at his sheep. They were in the big field, under the old elm trees.

"Yes," said he, "their wool must be cut. The warm days are coming, and the sheep will suffer if the wool is not cut off."

The next morning Mr. Bailey and his men went again to the field. They drove the sheep down to a little river. The men caught the sheep as they were thrown into the water, and washed the wool with their hands.

When the wool was clean and dry, the men cut it off with large shears. Soon many baskets were filled with fine white wool. It was then made into large bundles, and Mr. Bailey sent it to a woolen mill.

When it reached the mill, it was carded, spun, and woven into cloth.

Write a short composition, telling what you know about wool.

LESSON 128

AN ANSWER TO A NOTE OF INVITATION

Gladys Taylor has invited Edith Morton to her birthday party next Saturday afternoon. Edith expects to go to the country on that day, to visit her cousin, and so cannot accept the invitation.

Write Edith's answer to Gladys.

LESSON 129

OBSERVATION LESSON

Tell —

Five uses of wood.	Three uses of glass.
Three uses of leather.	Five uses of fire.
Five uses of iron.	Three uses of rubber.
Three uses of silver.	Five uses of electricity.
Three uses of gold.	Some uses of water.

LESSON 130

REPRODUCTION — ORAL AND WRITTEN

THE FOX AND THE STORK

Once a fox and a stork were good friends. The fox invited the stork to dinner. All they had to eat was soup. It was in flat dishes. The stork could put only the tip of his bill into the dish. The fox lapped his soup up quickly.

The next day the stork invited the fox to dinner. They had soup again. This time it was in a bottle. The stork could put his bill in and drink it, but the fox could only lick the outside of the bottle.

LESSON 131

SELECTION TO BE MEMORIZED

DISCONTENT

Down in a field, one day in June,
    The flowers all bloomed together
Save one, who tried to hide herself,
    And drooped that pleasant weather.

A robin, who had flown too high,
    And felt a little lazy,
Was resting near this buttercup
    Who wished she were a daisy.

For daisies grow so trig and tall!
    She always had a passion
For wearing frills around her neck,
    In just the daisies' fashion.

And buttercups must always be
    The same old tiresome color,
While daisies dress in gold and white,
    Although their gold is duller.

"Dear robin," said this sad young flower,
　"Perhaps you'd not mind trying
To find a nice white frill for me
　Some day, when you are flying?"

"You silly thing!" the robin said,
　"I think you must be crazy.
I'd rather be my honest self
　Than any made-up daisy.

"You're nicer in your own bright gown;
　The little children love you;
Be the best buttercup you can,
　And think no flower above you.

"Though swallows leave me out of sight,
　We'd better keep our places.
Perhaps the world would all go wrong
　Were there too many daisies.

"Look bravely up into the sky,
　And be content with knowing
That God wished for a buttercup
　Just here where you are growing."
　　　　　— SARAH ORNE JEWETT

LESSON 132

SENTENCE—STATEMENT—QUESTION

1. Where did the buttercup grow?
2. It grew in a field.
3. A robin was resting there.
4. What did the buttercup wish?
5. The buttercup wished to be a daisy.

A group of words that expresses a thought is a *sentence*.

With what kind of letter does each sentence begin?

How many of the above sentences *tell* something?

A sentence that tells something is a *statement*.

What mark of punctuation is placed after each statement?

How many of the above sentences ask something?

A sentence that asks something is a *question*.

What mark of punctuation is placed after a question?

Copy five statements from your reader.
Copy five questions from your reader.
Write five statements about the picture on page 110.
Write five questions about the picture on page 98.

LESSON 133

COMPOSITION

How Arthur Helped

Arthur Dale was the only child of a poor widow. His mother had to work very hard to earn a living for herself and her little boy.

Arthur was ten years old. He wished very much to help his mother.

Copy these two paragraphs and finish the story, telling what Arthur did to earn some money, how much he earned, when he worked, and how the money was spent.

LESSON 134

REPRODUCTION — ORAL AND WRITTEN

SAINT VALENTINE

A long time ago there lived a good old man named Valentine. He took care of people when they were sick, and helped them when they were sad or in trouble. He loved the children, and they loved him.

When he could not go to see the sick people or the children, he wrote loving letters to them.

Because he was so good and kind, everyone called him Saint Valentine.

On Saint Valentine's birthday we send kind messages to our friends. We call these messages, valentines.

LESSON 135

OBSERVATION LESSON — ORAL AND WRITTEN

You have watched buildings while they were being constructed; fill the following blanks, telling what these different workmen do; arrange the sentences in the order in which the work is done.

The painters _____
The excavators _____
The plumbers _____
The decorators _____
The stone masons _____
The lathers _____
The bricklayers _____
The plasterers _____
The carpenters _____

LESSON 136

THIS — THAT — THESE — THOSE

Copy these sentences and fill the blanks with *this, that, these,* or *those*:

1. _____ tree is an elm and _____ one is a maple.
2. _____ books are mine and _____ are yours.
3. _____ flower in my hand is blue.
4. I think _____ birds have a nest in the tree.

5. _____ apple you gave me is sour.

6. Did you buy many apples like _____ one?

7. The children like to read in _____ new books.

8. _____ book I am reading is interesting.

9. _____ horses are running away.

10. _____ knife is dull. May I borrow _____

Use **this** or **that** in speaking of _____ thing.

Use **these** or **those** in speaking of _____ _____ _____ thing.

Use _____ or _____ in speaking of what is near.

Use _____ or _____ in speaking of what is farther away.

LESSON 137

Use these words in sentences:

1. see	5. by	9. new
2. sea	6. buy	10. knew
3. here	7. right	11. fir
4. hear	8. write	12. fur

LESSON 138

LETTER WRITING

                              Denver, Colorado
                              Sept. 19, 1911

Dear Grace,

Our class is going to visit the children's ward at the hospital, Saturday afternoon, and we want you to go with us. We are going to take flowers, fruit, and books to the children. Let us know if we may expect you and what you will bring.

                         Your loving friend,
                         Florence Bailey.

Write the answer to Florence's letter.

LESSON 139

SELECTION FOR MEMORIZING

THE VIOLET

Dear little Violet,
   Don't be afraid!
Lift your blue eyes
   From the rock's mossy shade!

All the birds call for you
Out of the sky.
May is here waiting,
And here, too, am I.

Why do you shiver so,
Violet sweet?
Soft is the meadow-grass
Under my feet.
Wrapped in your hood of green,
Violet, why
Peep from your earth door
So silent and shy?

Trickle the little brooks
Close to your bed;
Softest of fleecy clouds
Float overhead.
"Ready and waiting!"
The slender reeds sigh.
"Ready and waiting!"
We sing — May and I.

Come, pretty Violet,
Winter's away;

Come, for without you
    May isn't May.
Down through the sunshine
    Wings flutter and fly:
Quick, little Violet,
    Open your eye!

Hear the rain whisper,
    "Dear Violet, come!"
How can you stay
    In your underground home?
Up in the pine boughs
    For you the winds sigh,
Homesick to see you
    Are we, May and I.

Ha! though you care not
    For call or for shout,
Yon troop of sunbeams
    Are winning you out.
Now all is beautiful
    Under the sky,
May's here — and violets!
    Winter, good-bye!

—LUCY LARCOM

From a painting by Millet.

FEEDING HER BIRDS

LESSON 140

A PICTURE LESSON

What is the name of this picture?
Why did the artist give it this name?
How many little girls do you see?
Which one do you think has just been fed?
Whose turn will come next?

Write a story about the picture.

LESSON 141

REPRODUCTION

THE GREEK MYTH OF NARCISSUS

Narcissus had a twin sister whom he dearly loved. This sister died when she was young. Narcissus was lonesome. He missed his sister who was so pretty.

One day he stood by the side of a spring, thinking of his sister. As he looked down into the water, he saw a face like hers looking up at him.

Of course the face he saw was really the reflection of his own, but he did not know that.

He thought his sister must have been changed to a water fairy and was there looking at him.

He came to the spring day after day, until at last the gods felt sorry for him and changed him to a flower.

This flower was the beautiful narcissus. When these flowers grow beside a pond or a stream, they bend their pretty heads and look at the reflection of their faces in the water.

Read this story several times; close your book and write it.

LESSON 142

Fill these blanks with words from the list at the end of the lesson:

1. One who writes books is an _____.
2. One who paints pictures is an _____.
3. One who draws plans for buildings is an _____.
4. A man who fights in the army is a _____.
5. A _____ is one who makes music.
6. A _____ takes care of sheep.
7. A _____ writes poetry.

8. Men who sail ships are _____.
9. One who studies is a _____.
10. A _____ builds houses.
11. A _____ makes men's clothes.
12. A _____ makes ladies' clothes.
13. A _____ makes ladies' hats.
14. A man who runs an engine is an _____.

architect	artist	student
milliner	dressmaker	poet
author	soldier	shepherd
tailor	carpenter	musician
sailor	engineer	

LESSON 143

OBSERVATION LESSON — ORAL

Foods

1. Name plants whose roots are used for food.
2. Name plants whose stalks are used for food.
3. Name plants whose leaves are used for food.

4. Name plants whose flowers are used for food.

5. Name plants whose seeds are used for food.

6. What foods grow on trees?

7. What foods grow in large fields?

8. What foods grow on vines?

9. What foods grow in gardens?

10. What foods are eaten raw?

11. What foods require cooking?

12. From what animals do we get mutton?

13. From what animals do we get beef? Veal? Pork?

14. From what animals do we get venison?

15. What other animals furnish us with food?

LESSON 144

LETTER WRITING

RALPH TO HAROLD

Ralph is going away for the summer and wants to know if Harold will take care of his pony, Rex, for him, while he is gone. He will bring Rex on

Saturday, if Harold's mother is willing.

Write the letter for Ralph.

LESSON 145

LETTER WRITING

HAROLD TO RALPH

Harold will be delighted to care for Rex. His mother invites Ralph to come and spend the day, Saturday. Ralph can bring Rex and show Harold how a pony should be taken care of.

Write the letter for Harold.

LESSON 146

CONVERSATION LESSON

If you had a piece of land on which you could plant anything you wished, —
What kind of shade trees would you plant? Where would you put them?
What kind of shrubs would you select?

What kind of fruit trees?

Would you want any berry bushes? What kind?

Where would you place a grape arbor?

Would you want any nut trees? What kind?

What kinds of flowers and vines would you have?

What vegetables would you have in the garden?

How would you prepare the ground for a garden?

Draw a diagram, showing the best place for a house, and marking places for the trees, shrubs, berry bushes, and garden.

LESSON 147

SELECTION FOR MEMORIZING

A Boy's Song

Where the pools are bright and deep
Where the gray trout lies asleep,
Up the river and o'er the lea,
That's the way for Billy and me.

Where the blackbird sings the latest,
Where the hawthorn blooms the sweetest,
Where the nestlings chirp and flee,
That's the way for Billy and me.

Where the mowers mow the cleanest,
Where the hay lies thick and greenest,
There to track the homeward bee,
That's the way for Billy and me.

Where the hazel bank is steepest,
Where the shadow falls the deepest,
Where the clustering nuts fall free,
That's the way for Billy and me.

Why the boys should drive away
Little sweet maidens from the play,
Or love to banter and fight so well,
That's the thing I never could tell.

But this I know — I love to play,
Through the meadow, among the hay;
Up the water and o'er the lea;
That's the way for Billy and me.

— James Hogg

LESSON 148

INFORMATION LESSON

Bees

What is the home of the bees called?

How many kinds of bees are there? (Workers, drones, and queens.)

How many queens can live in each hive?

What does the queen do?

What happens if the queen bee dies?

How do the workers keep busy?

How many sides has each cell?

Name two uses for these cells.

How does a bee carry pollen?

What use is made of the pollen?

In what way do the bees help the flowers?

How do the bees defend themselves?

What enemies have the bees?

LESSON 149

Write sentences containing these words:

1. sun	3. fore	5. flour	7. hare
2. son	4. four	6. flower	8. hair

LESSON 150

REPRODUCTION — ORAL AND WRITTEN

THE GOLDEN TOUCH

According to Greek mythology, there was once a king named Midas. This king had a little daughter whose name was Marygold.

Now Midas loved gold more than anything else. One day a fairy gave him the golden touch. Then everything that he touched turned to gold.

At first the king was very happy. Roses and lilies became gold when he touched them.

As he was walking in the garden, his little girl came running to meet him. He stooped to kiss her and immediately she became a golden statue.

Then the king begged the fairy to take away the golden touch and give him his Marygold again. The fairy was sorry for him. She told him to bathe in the river and sprinkle some of the water on his little girl.

He hurried to do as the fairy had said, and soon he held his little daughter again in his arms.

LESSON 151

LETTER WRITING

Write a note from Nellie Martin to Cora Arnold, asking her to go for an automobile ride, next Saturday afternoon, with Nellie and Nellie's Uncle Ben. Tell her that they will take their lunch with them and will not return until late.

LESSON 152

Write sentences containing the following words:

1. see	7. go	13. sing
2. saw	8. went	14. sang
3. have seen	9. have gone	15. have sung
or	or	or
has seen	has gone	has sung
4. break	10. draw	16. write
5. broke	11. drew	17. wrote
6. have broken	12. have drawn	18. have written
or	or	or
has broken	has drawn	has written

LESSON 153

CONVERSATION LESSON

ANIMALS

1. What animal is called the "king of beasts"?

2. Name three useful animals. Name three harmful animals.

3. Name an animal that supplies us with warm clothing.

4. Name three animals that are called "beasts of burden."

5. Name some animals that are valuable for their fur.

6. How does a dog defend itself?

7. How does a deer defend itself?

8. How does a snake defend itself?

9. What is the largest animal you have seen?

10. What animals store away food for winter?

11. What animal has a very long neck?

12. Name an animal from which ivory is obtained.

13. What animal cuts down trees by gnawing them with its sharp front teeth?

14. Name four kinds of fish.

15. Name a kind of fish that has no scales.

LESSON 154

LETTER WRITING

Springfield, Illinois
March 30, 1909

Dear Cousin Ben,

When I visited you in the country last summer, you promised to send me some shrubs and other plants for my flower beds this spring. Please send them by express and I will pay the charges here.

Can't you come to see us some time soon?

Your loving cousin,
Henry Thayer.

Write the letter which Cousin Ben sends with the package, telling the names of the plants and giving instructions about caring for them. Tell when Ben is coming to the city.

LESSON 155

CONVERSATION LESSON

How are our homes lighted?

How were houses lighted many years ago?

How were candles made?

Describe a coal-oil lamp. How many parts has it? Of what use is the chimney?

Where does gas come from? How is it carried to a house?

How is gaslight put out? What happens if it is blown out?

How is electricity brought into homes? How are electric lamps lighted? How is the light put out?

LESSON 156

REPRODUCTION — ORAL AND WRITTEN

THE MYTH OF THE SUNFLOWER

Once there was a little girl named Clytie. She had long golden hair and she always wore a green dress.

Her home was not on land. It was in the sea. She had a pretty carriage drawn by four goldfishes.

One day she drove them to the top of the water. She stepped from her carriage and sat down on a rock near the shore. She looked up at the sky and saw the great sun. Clytie had never seen him before, and she watched him all day, until he went down in the west.

Early the next morning she came again to see him. She thought he was so beautiful and so wonderful that she wished to be like him.

Every day she came to watch him, and every evening she felt sad when he disappeared.

But one night, when she started to go home, she could not move her feet. They had turned to roots. Her green dress was a stalk, her arms were leaves, and her beautiful yellow hair had turned to petals.

The next morning, when the sun arose, he saw a tall and stately flower standing by the seaside. It watched him all day, turning its head as he went from east to west.

"It is my flower," said the sun. "Because it loves me so, it shall have my name and shall be called the 'sunflower.'"

LESSON 157

SELECTION TO BE MEMORIZED

THE SANDMAN

The rosy clouds float overhead,
  The sun is going down;
And now the sandman's gentle tread
  Comes stealing through the town.
"White sand, white sand," he softly cries,
  And as he shakes his hand,
Straightway there lies on babies' eyes
  His gift of shining sand.
Blue eyes, gray eyes, black eyes, and brown,
As shuts the rose, they softly close, when he
  goes through the town.

From sunny beaches far away —
  Yes, in another land —
He gathers up at break of day
  His store of shining sand.
No tempests beat that shore remote,
  No ships may sail that way;
His little boat alone may float
  Within that lovely bay.

Blue eyes, gray eyes, black eyes, and brown,
As shuts the rose, they softly close, when he
    goes through the town.

He smiles to see the eyelids close
    Above the happy eyes;
And every child right well he knows, —
    Oh, he is very wise!
But if, as he goes through the land,
    A naughty baby cries,
His other hand takes dull gray sand
    To close the wakeful eyes.
Blue eyes, gray eyes, black eyes, and brown,
As shuts the rose, they softly close, when he
    goes through the town.

So, when you hear the sandman's song
    Sound through the twilight sweet,
Be sure you do not keep him long
    Awaiting on the street.
Lie softly down, dear little head,
    Rest quiet, busy hands,
Till on your bed, his good night said,
    He strews the shining sands.

Blue eyes, gray eyes, black eyes, and brown,
As shuts the rose, they softly close, when he
goes through the town.

— MARGARET VANDEGRIFT

Write the first stanza of this poem from memory.

LESSON 158

Copy these sentences and fill the blanks with *hasn't* or *haven't:*

1. Bessie _____ any new dress.
2. Tom and Frank _____ any ball.
3. The poor boy _____ any overcoat.
4. We _____ seen the new pictures.
5. Will's dog _____ any collar.
6. The wind _____ blown today.
7. They _____ asked us to go.
8. I _____ finished my lesson.
9. My brother _____ a pencil.
10. I _____ any pencil, either.
11. _____ you a pen?
12. Jack will have to go without his lunch, for he _____ any money.

LESSON 159

BIRDS

What bird is called the "King of Birds"?

What bird weaves its nest, hanging it in a tree?

What bird pecks a hole in a tree for its nest?

Name three birds that are sweet singers.

Name three birds that cannot sing.

What big bird can run as fast as a horse?

What bird makes a humming noise when it flies?

Name three birds that can swim.

What bird builds its nest in a chimney?

What bird lays its eggs in other birds' nests?

Name three birds that have hooked bills.
Name three birds with webbed feet.
What bird sleeps in the daytime?
Name two birds smaller than the robin.

LESSON 160

LETTER WRITING

St. Paul, Minnesota
April 24, 1910

Dear Cousin Edith,

Your letter was received a few days ago, and we are glad to know that you are well again.

Can't you make us a visit this spring? It is nearly a year since you were here, and we all want to see you. I am sure a change would do you good. School will be out soon, and then we can ride old Don and have many good times together.

Write to me soon and tell me that you will come.

Your loving cousin,
Ethel Edwards.

From a painting by Olivie.

ANXIETY

Write Edith's reply to the letter, saying that she cannot visit her cousin this spring, and telling the reason why. She thanks Ethel for the kind invitation, and hopes to be able to visit her early in the fall. Tell about the close of school and Edith's plans for the summer.

LESSON 161

A PICTURE LESSON

What has the little girl in her hand?
Do you think she is afraid of the dog?
What would the dog say if he could talk?
Write a story about the picture.

LESSON 162

FOR COPYING AND DISCUSSION

MAXIMS AND PROVERBS

1. We can do more good by being good than in any other way.
2. To be good is the mother of to do good.
3. The secret of being lovely is being unselfish.

4. Write it on your heart that every day is the best day of the year.

5. Early to bed, early to rise,
   Makes a man healthy, wealthy, and wise.

6. A good beginning makes a good ending.

7. Do to others as you would that others should do to you.

8. Whatever is worth doing at all is worth doing well.

9. Where there is a will there is a way.

10. A stitch in time saves nine.

11. A good name is rather to be chosen than great riches.

12. Think before you speak.

13. A soft answer turneth away wrath.

14. Honesty is the best policy.

15. A penny saved is a penny earned.

16. Many hands make light work.

LESSON 163

COMPOSITION

Write a story illustrating one of the maxims or proverbs given in Lesson 162.

LESSON 164

SELECTION TO BE MEMORIZED

COLUMBIA, THE GEM OF THE OCEAN

O Columbia! the gem of the ocean,
The home of the brave and the free,
The shrine of each patriot's devotion
A world offers homage to thee.
Thy mandates make heroes assemble,
When Liberty's form stands in view;
Thy banners make Tyranny tremble,
When borne by the red, white, and blue.

When war winged its wide desolation
And threatened the land to deform,
The ark, then, of freedom's foundation,
Columbia, rode safe through the storm,
With her garlands of vict'ry around her,
When so proudly she bore her brave crew,
With her flag proudly floating before her,
The boast of the red, white, and blue.

The star-spangled banner bring hither,
O'er Columbia's true sons let it wave;

May the wreaths they have won never wither,
Nor its stars cease to shine on the brave.
May the service united ne'er sever,
But they to their colors hold true!
The Army and Navy forever,
Three cheers for the red, white, and blue!

— David T. Shaw

Books Available from
Lost Classics Book Company

American History
Stories of Great Americans for Little Americans...Edward Eggleston
A First Book in American History .... Edward Eggleston
A History of the United States and Its People........ Edward Eggleston

Biography
The Life of Kit Carson .... Edward Ellis

English Grammar
Primary Language Lessons.. Emma Serl
Intermediate Language Lessons...................................... Emma Serl

Historical Fiction
With Lee in Virginia .... G. A. Henty
A Tale of the Western Plains .... G. A. Henty
The Young Carthaginian .... G. A. Henty
In the Heart of the Rockies.. G. A. Henty
For the Temple .... G. A. Henty
A Knight of the White Cross .... G. A. Henty
The Minute Boys of Lexington.......................... Edward Stratemeyer
The Minute Boys of Bunker Hill........................ Edward Stratemeyer
Hope and Have .... Oliver Optic
Taken by the Enemy, First in *The Blue and the Gray Series* .... Oliver Optic
Within the Enemy's Lines, Second in *The Blue and the Gray Series* .. Oliver Optic
On the Blockade, Third in *The Blue and the Gray Series* .... Oliver Optic
Stand by the Union, Fourth in *The Blue and the Gray Series* .... Oliver Optic
Mary of Plymouth .... James Otis

To Order or Request a Catalog
Telephone: (888) 611-BOOK *(2665)*
Postal Requests: Lost Classics Book Company
                  P. O. Box 1756, Ft. Collins, CO 80522
Please send a catalog and order form to:

Company name: _____

Name: _____

Address:_____

City: _____

State:_____   Zip:_____-_____

Telephone: (   ) _____